BABY MEMORIES

Parents:

Date of Birth

Other Baby Facts

Made in the USA
Monee, IL
22 September 2022

14446750R00072